Why Science Matters

Using Nuclear Energy

John Townsend

www.raintreepublishers.co.uk
Visit our website to find out
more information about
Raintree books.

To order:
☎ Phone 0845 6044371
▤ Fax +44 (0) 1865 312263
▧ Email myorders@capstonepub.co.uk

Customers from outside the UK please telephone +44 1865 312262

Raintree is an imprint of Capstone Global Library Limited, a company incorporated in England and Wales having its registered office at 7 Pilgrim Street, London, EC4V 6LB – Registered company number: 6695582

"Raintree" is a registered trademark of Pearson Education Limited, under licence to Capstone Global Library Limited

Text © Capstone Global Library Limited
First published in hardback in 2009
Paperback edition first published in 2010
The moral rights of the proprietor have been asserted.

Edited by Pollyanna Poulter and Rebecca Vickers
Designed by Steven Mead and Q2A Creative Solutions
Original illustrations © Capstone Global Library Limited by
    Gordon Hurden
Picture research by Ruth Blair
Production by Victoria Fitzgerald
Originated by Heinemann Library
Printed and bound in China by Leo Paper Group.

British Library Cataloguing-in-Publication Data
Townsend, John, 1955-
Using nuclear energy. - (Why science matters)
1. Nuclear energy - Juvenile literature 2. Nuclear engineering - Juvenile literature
I. Title
621.4'8
A full catalogue record for this book is available from the British Library.

Acknowledgements
We would like to thank the following for permission to reproduce photographs: © Corbis pp. **20** (Wang Jianmin/Xinhua Press), **22**; © Ford Motor Company p. **23**; © Istockphoto background images and design features; © PA Photos pp. **7** (AP/Toby Talbot), **17** (AP/Carolyn Kaster), **19** (AP/Koji Sasahara), **28** (AP/James MacPherson), **45** (AP/Eyepress); © Photodisc p. **41** (StockTrek); © Photolibrary p. **36** (Phototake Science); © published with permission of ITER p. **44**; © Science Photo Library pp. **4** (Prof.Peter Fowler), **9** (Los Alamos National Laboratory), **10** (US Navy), **13** (US Dept of Energy), **14** (Patrick Landmann), **18** (Ria Novosti), **25** (Medi-Mation), **30** (Jim Amos), **31** (James King-Holmes), **32** (Steve Allen), **33** (US Dept of Energy), **34** and **38** (Gustoimages), **35** (Zephyr), **37** (Martin Dohrn), **39** (Chris Priest), **43** (Philippe Plailly/Eurelios), **46** (Carl Goodman).

Cover photograph of a Power Burst Facility (PBF) test at Sandia reproduced with permission of © Corbis/Karen Kasmauski.

We would like to thank John Pucek for his invaluable help in the preparation of this book.

Every effort has been made to contact copyright holders of material reproduced in this book. Any omissions will be rectified in subsequent printings if notice is given to the Publishers.

Disclaimer
All the Internet addresses (URLs) given in this book were valid at the time of going to press. However, due to the dynamic nature of the Internet, some addresses may have changed, or sites may have changed or ceased to exist since publication. While the author and Publishers regret any inconvenience this may cause readers, no responsibility for any such changes can be accepted by either the author or the Publishers.

Contents

Some words are printed in bold, **like this**. You can find out what they mean in the glossary.

Understanding atoms

Since the early 19th century, scientists have known that all matter is made up of simple particles called **atoms**. However, it wasn't until the beginning of the 20th century that scientists realized atoms could be "split". By changing the structure of an atom, scientists can release massive amounts of energy.

Britain's Joseph Thomson and New Zealand's Ernest Rutherford made some of the most important discoveries about atoms and nuclear physics in the 1890s. Thomson described atoms as being like "plum puddings" because he believed they contained even smaller particles, like currants inside a cake. Rutherford also studied the structure of individual atoms. Their work, along with the ideas of Denmark's Niels Bohr, helped scientists to understand atomic structure. From this knowledge, scientists developed the idea of breaking up and changing atoms to release a powerful source of energy. They called it nuclear **fission**.

Some of the top scientists of 1911 met at the Solvay Conference, including Albert Einstein (first on the left, standing), Marie Curie (second from left, seated), and Ernest Rutherford (standing behind Marie Curie).

Big ideas

In the early 1900s, another great scientist was at work. His name was Albert Einstein, and his ideas were to change physics forever. Einstein developed a theory about the nature of the universe that had a great impact on our understanding of energy. Because of his work, experiments in nuclear physics took off in new directions.

Albert Einstein (1879–1955)

Albert Einstein is considered by many scientists to have been the greatest physicist of the last century. He was born in Germany and worked in Switzerland and the USA. His work changed our understanding of time and space, and he developed theories used to build models of the universe. In 1905, Einstein developed his theory of relativity, which showed that energy and **mass** are really different aspects of the same thing. Matter can be turned into energy, and energy into matter, as shown in his famous formula:

$$E=mc^2$$
(E = energy, m = mass, c = the speed of light)

According to Einstein, if we could change mass into energy, it would be possible to let loose huge amounts of heat. For example, just 30 grams of hydrogen atoms could release as much heat as burning hundreds of thousands of litres of oil. The results of Einstein's thinking were revolutionary and would prove to be an earth-shattering introduction to nuclear energy.

Today, nuclear energy generates clean, low-cost electricity, powers some of the world's largest ships, creates the most destructive weapons on Earth, and enables the latest life-saving healthcare technology. It is life-changing science that affects us all.

Fission

In the early 1930s, scientists identified the particles that make up atoms and the forces that hold them together. Particles called **electrons** move around an atom's **nucleus**, and there are also particles that make up the nucleus itself. Scientists called these small particles **protons** and **neutrons**. For example, the simplest atom is hydrogen, which has a nucleus containing one proton circled by one moving electron. The next simplest atom, helium, has a nucleus with two protons and two neutrons circled by two electrons. The number of protons in an atom determines what **element** it is.

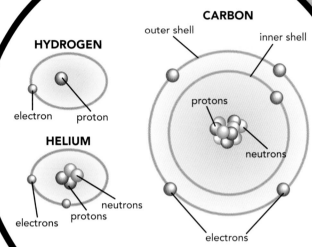

Breakthrough

Scientists realized that every atom has electrical energy because the moving electrons have a negative electrical charge. Protons have a positive electrical charge and neutrons, being neutral, have no charge at all. Experiments showed that there were forces inside every atom controlling the moving electrons, as well as holding the protons together. The big question was whether this energy inside atoms could be harnessed and used in some way. Nuclear energy is released by changing the nucleus of an atom. These changes are called **nuclear reactions**. The heat created in a nuclear reaction is known as atomic energy, but it is more commonly called nuclear energy.

Though atoms are made up almost entirely of empty space, the main parts are: electrons, and the protons and neutrons of the nucleus. Today, scientists think that protons and neutrons are made of even smaller particles called **quarks.**

Splitting the atom

Nuclear reactions are a natural process. The Sun and other stars make heat and light by nuclear reactions. However, since the mid 20th century, scientists have been able to create nuclear reactions artificially. In 1938, two German scientists, Otto Hahn and Fritz Strassman, along with Lise Meitner of Austria, discovered that they could split the nucleus of an atom in half by bombarding it with neutrons. As the nucleus split, some of its mass was converted into heat energy. This splitting of the atom, known as nuclear fission, was the start of a new and potentially dangerous branch of science, the possibilities of which had never before been understood.

Engineers load special fuel rods inside a nuclear reactor where fission will take place.

THE SCIENCE YOU LEARN: ESSENTIAL ELEMENTS

Everything in the universe is made up of atoms. Each type of atom makes an element, such as gold or oxygen. There are 92 naturally occurring elements. Your body contains trillions of atoms, and 25–26 elements that are essential for life. So inside our body tissues are atoms of hydrogen and oxygen, carbon and nitrogen, as well as atoms of calcium, zinc, iron, and even phosphorus!

Using uranium

Uranium is an element found in most rocks and in Earth's crust. It was first discovered in 1789 and named after the planet Uranus, which had been discovered eight years earlier. But scientists discovered something special about uranium atoms. They are bigger than most other atoms and the nucleus contains many protons and neutrons. In fact, a uranium atom is the heaviest of all the naturally occurring elements, with an atomic number of 92. This means that there are 92 protons contained in the atom's nucleus, which is a huge amount when compared with lighter elements, such as hydrogen (with an atomic number 1), and oxygen (with an atomic number of 8).

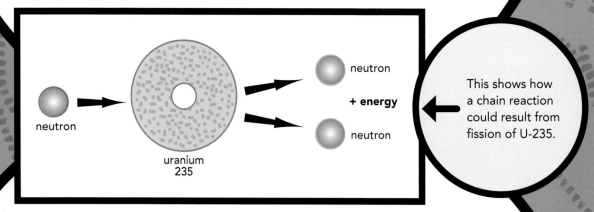

neutron

+ energy

neutron

neutron

uranium
235

This shows how a chain reaction could result from fission of U-235.

The most common type of uranium found in rock, soil, and water is called U-238. But the type of uranium that creates a nuclear reaction is called U-235. This number refers to the protons and neutrons in each atom. As well as its 92 protons, this type of uranium atom contains 143 neutrons. As 92 + 143 = 235, the uranium atom is named U-235. U-235 is an **isotope** that releases high energy particles or waves. Such energy can detach electrons (known as **ionizing**), causing "ionizing **radiation**". In other words, uranium is **radioactive**.

In the late 1930s, Enrico Fermi and other scientists noticed that uranium atoms were unstable because they fell apart easily. They broke up into smaller atoms and released energy. Not only that, but when the nucleus of a uranium atom was split in the laboratory it gave off more neutrons, which could in turn split other uranium atoms. Fermi believed that in the correct conditions this would start a **chain reaction**. If this happens over and over again, many millions of times, a very large amount of heat could be produced from a small amount of uranium. Scientists realized that this process of nuclear fission could produce enormous amounts of energy, just by using uranium atoms. Enrico Fermi received a **Nobel Prize** in 1938 for the discovery of nuclear chain reactions, and Otto Hahn won the Nobel Prize in 1944 for the discovery of nuclear fission.

Knock-on effect

When a nuclear chain reaction occurs, the split atom will also give off two or three of its "spare" neutrons, which fly out with such force they can split any other atoms that they hit. As such, it is only necessary to split just one U-235 atom. The neutrons firing from it will split other atoms, which in turn will split more, then more ... and so on. This chain reaction will happen within a millionth of a second, releasing great energy.

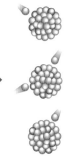

1. Neutron strikes unstable nucleus of U-235.

2. Nucleus splits, releasing large amount of energy.

3. Further neutrons are released.

4. New neutrons strike other nuclei, initiating a chain reaction.

Scientists in New Mexico, USA, researched and developed the world's first atom bomb during 1945. Left to right here are E.O. Lawrence, Enrico Fermi, and I.I. Rabi.

The neutrons that are released when an atom splits fly out with such force that they cause more atoms to be split, leading to a chain reaction.

In the 1940s, the new physics of nuclear fission and chain reactions was exciting scientists around the world. But this was during World War II and scientists faced a problem. Nuclear chain reactions could be controlled to produce electricity, but they could also be allowed to speed up, get out of control, and cause massive explosions. The country that made the first massive bomb by releasing neutrons could effectively win the war. Uranium atoms and nuclear energy could be used to kill millions of people. There were tough choices ahead.

The bomb

In August 1939, Albert Einstein wrote a letter to the American President, Franklin D. Roosevelt, urging the USA to start a nuclear program without delay: "*It may become possible to set up nuclear chain reactions in a large mass of uranium ... This new phenomenon would also lead to the construction of bombs ... A single bomb of this type, carried by boat or exploded in a port, might very well destroy the whole port, together with some of the surrounding territory*".

In later years, Einstein regretted sending the letter and called it the greatest mistake of his life. He became appalled by the development of nuclear weapons and their terrifying power. However, President Roosevelt followed Einstein's advice. During World War II, scientists in the USA, Canada, and the UK worked to develop an atomic bomb. There were many initial problems in getting the reaction to work effectively but, after a successful test of a bomb in the New Mexico desert, an atomic bomb was dropped on Hiroshima in Japan. The sudden power it unleashed was shocking. Within minutes of a U.S. plane dropping the bomb, it detonated in Hiroshima and created a white-hot glare that lit the sky and blasted fierce winds. From a huge fireball (a quarter of a mile across) rose a mushroom-shaped cloud that reached up to 10,000 metres (32,800 feet) in the sky. The intense heat was perhaps as much as 3,000°C (5,400°F). Thousands of buildings blew apart from the blast. A survivor described a blinding flash across the sky, followed by scorching heat, dead silence, and then a huge "boom" like the rumbling of distant thunder.

Approximately 200,000 people died from the Hiroshima bomb and its aftermath. This bomb, as well as another atomic bomb dropped on Nagasaki in Japan, caused the Japanese government to surrender and World War II came to an end.

The vast, mushroom-shaped cloud from an atomic bomb.

Explosive science

The massive power released when an atomic bomb explodes comes from the strong nuclear force inside the atoms. Within a fraction of a second, all the nuclei have been hit by escaping neutrons and have broken down. The extra energy, in trillions of atomic nuclei, is all released at once. The explosion of a nuclear bomb is like 40,000 normal bombs exploding in the same place, at the same time.

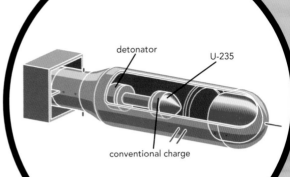

There are two main types of bomb that release energy from the nuclei of atoms. The simplest model is like "Little Boy" (see right and below). The more complicated type is the hydrogen bomb, or thermonuclear bomb. This releases an even greater quantity of energy through a process called **nuclear fusion** (see page 40).

A lot of today's nuclear bombs have ten times the force of the Little Boy bomb and many countries now have nuclear weapons – a matter of continuing worldwide concern.

The design of "Little Boy", in which there is a conventional charge.

CASE STUDY

Little Boy

The project to develop the first nuclear weapon during World War II was called the Manhattan Project. American physicist J. Robert Oppenheimer directed the research, done by scientists. Their result was an atomic bomb with the code-name "Little Boy". It was about 3 m (10 ft) in length, about 70 cm (28 in) in diameter, and weighed around 4,100 kg (9,000 lb). Inside, it had a mechanism that fired one mass of U-235 at another mass of U-235. Once the two pieces of uranium met, the released neutrons travelled at speeds of about 10 million metres per second. The sudden burst of neutrons triggered the chain reaction, which continued until the energy released became so great that the bomb blew itself apart. "Little Boy" was dropped on Hiroshima on 6 August 1945.

Nuclear power

The new and shocking power released from the nuclei of atoms astonished the world. The terrible destruction caused by atomic bombs made everyone fear nuclear energy. So the challenge for scientists was to prove that the science behind such destruction could be turned into a power for good.

Nuclear fuel

In the last 50 years, uranium has become one of the world's most important energy minerals. Traces of it occur almost everywhere, including in the world's oceans. There are uranium mines in about 20 countries, although more than two-thirds of world production comes from just 10 mines. Today, there are strict controls on the buying and selling of uranium. It is only sold to countries that have signed the Nuclear Non-Proliferation Treaty. This allows international inspectors to check that it is used only for peaceful purposes.

	Tonnes	% of world
1. Australia	1,143,000	24%
2. Kazakhstan	816,000	17%
3. Canada	444,000	9%
4. U.S.	342,000	7%
5. South Africa	341,000	7%
6. Namibia	282,000	6%
7. Brazil	279,000	6%
8. Niger	225,000	5%
9. Russia	172,000	4%
10. Uzbekistan	116,000	2%
11. Ukraine	90,000	2%
12. Jordan	79,000	2%
13. India	67,000	1%
14. China	60,000	1%
15. Other	287,000	7%

This table shows which countries have the largest uranium resources and the percentage of uranium they have in relation to that of the whole world.

Uranium: from Earth to energy

Uranium is mined from underground and the **ore** is crushed and extracted. Before it is used as a fuel, it has to be "enriched". This is because the fuel for nuclear **reactors** must have a higher concentration of U-235 than exists in natural uranium ore. U-235 is the key ingredient that starts a nuclear reaction and keeps it going. Enriching uranium increases the amount of the U-235 isotope by three to five percent. The enriched uranium is made into fuel pellets about the size of jellybeans. It is then placed in metal tubes and used in the reactor core to create nuclear fission. A handful of nuclear pellets provides as much electricity as 390 barrels of oil. A nuclear power station needs only 74kg of uranium pellets per day to generate 1,000 megawatts of electricity compared to the 8,600 tonnes of coal that would be required.

Plutonium

As well as being able to release energy from uranium atoms, scientists found another useful source of atomic nuclei in the fuel called **plutonium**. It was first used in the 1940s in nuclear weapons. Today, over one third of the energy produced in most nuclear electricity stations comes from plutonium, which is created there as a by-product of uranium. Only small traces of plutonium are found naturally. One of the ways in which it is obtained is from dismantled nuclear weapons, as well as from the used uranium in nuclear reactors.

In a single atom of the most stable type of plutonium (isotope 244), there are 94 protons and 150 neutrons. This arrangement of particles makes it even more suitable than uranium for nuclear fission and chain reaction. Plutonium makes a good nuclear fuel, but is very toxic and difficult to dispose of safely, so it must be dealt with extremely carefully. Despite the risks, plutonium creates much of today's electricity, so the next question is: how?

This is a pellet of glowing plutonium. Small amounts of plutonium are warm to the touch, but larger amounts can boil water.

Nuclear reactors

The real challenge, after making an explosive nuclear reaction, was to control all of the energy released from nuclear fission and use it to make safe electrical power. In the 1950s, scientists from the USA, UK, France, Canada, and the former Soviet Union were experimenting with reactors that could generate enough electricity to power large cities.

- 1951: an experimental reactor in Idaho, USA, produced the first usable electric power from splitting atoms, lighting four light bulbs.
- 1955: a U.S. town – Arco, in Idaho, with a population of 1,000 – was powered by nuclear energy.
- 1956: the world's first large-scale nuclear power station opened at Calder Hall in Cumbria.

Reactor type	Main countries	Numbers
Pressurized water reactor	USA, France, Japan, Russia	264
Boiling water reactor	USA, Japan, Sweden	94
Pressurized heavy water reactor	Canada	43
Gas-cooled reactor	UK	18
Light water graphite reactor	Russia	12
Fast neutron reactor	Japan, France, Russia	4
Other	Russia	4
	Total	439

Source: *Nuclear Engineering International Handbook 2007*
http://www.world-nuclear.org/info/inf32.html

This table shows how many different sorts of reactors were used by various nuclear power plants around the world in 2007. It is clear that the pressurized water reactor was the most common.

This is the enormous nuclear turbine steam generator in the Ardennes region of France, which began operating in 2000.

Although there are now over 400 large nuclear power stations of various designs around the world, most of them use reactors that produce and control the release of energy from splitting atoms of uranium or plutonium. The immense heat released from continuous fission of the atoms is used to make steam that drives **turbines** in order to produce electricity. The great advantages of nuclear-powered electricity over the old, coal-fired power stations are that they need less fuel, are cheaper to run, and produce hardly any greenhouse gases, such as carbon dioxide.

Reactor moderators

Controlled fission is achieved when the free neutrons in a reaction are slowed down. A substance called a moderator, which slows down the moving neutrons, surrounds fuel rods inside the reactor core. In the most common type of modern reactor, the pressurized water reactor (shown below), the moderator is water. As well as slowing the neutrons, the water cools the reactor and carries the heat away to make the steam that turns the turbines.

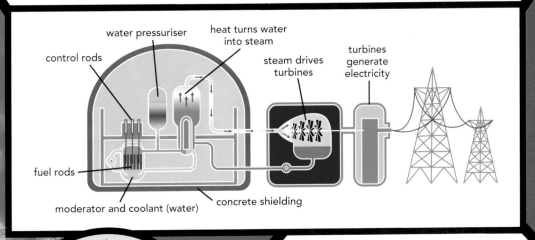

control rods

water pressuriser

heat turns water into steam

steam drives turbines

turbines generate electricity

fuel rods

moderator and coolant (water)

concrete shielding

This diagram of a pressurized water reactor shows how the nuclear reaction is transformed into electrical power.

In a controlled nuclear chain reaction, only one neutron should strike another atom. All around the reactor is a heavy concrete shield to stop radiation escaping. Modern reactors are designed to shut down if there is a problem, which stops them running out of control.

Risks

Although the latest nuclear power stations are built with many safety features, some people are concerned about the fuel they use. Making electricity from uranium and plutonium may mean that less coal is being burned, reducing the amount of smoke and carbon pollution, but there is still a risk to the environment from nuclear waste or leaks. Uranium that is spent (meaning it cannot be used again) is a very dangerous by-product of nuclear electricity.

Several stages of the nuclear fuel cycle create risks of radioactive leaks and produce dangerous waste.

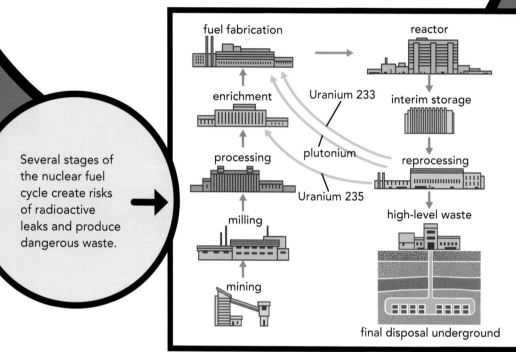

fuel fabrication   reactor

enrichment   Uranium 233   interim storage

processing   plutonium   reprocessing

Uranium 235

milling   high-level waste

mining

final disposal underground

Safe recycling

Some waste from nuclear reactors can be reused, which helps to reduce some of the risks. The nuclear fuel cycle (shown in the diagram above) starts with the mining of uranium, which then goes through stages of preparation before being used as fuel for the reactor. Some of the used uranium can then be recycled or made into plutonium for further fission. The final stages of the process involve the preparing, managing, and disposing of the highly radioactive, spent nuclear fuel.

Milling is the extracting of uranium from mined ore in rocks. After a concentrated **yellowcake** of uranium is produced at the mill, the next step is to convert it into pure uranium hexafluoride (UF_6) gas, suitable for use in enrichment operations. Manufacturing fuel can involve mixed oxide fuel, which is a combination of uranium and plutonium. Finally, reprocessing is the chemical operation carried out to separate the spent fuel that can be recycled from the waste that must be disposed of safely.

Early problems

One of the major first incidents in a power station happened in 1957. A fire at the Windscale reactor in the UK led to the release of harmful, radioactive material that spread across the UK and Europe. The reactor overheated because a failure of the graphite moderator (used to control the speed of the reaction) allowed a fire to get out of control. There was a real danger of **meltdown,** but the fire was eventually extinguished by shutting down the airflow. Although a serious explosion was avoided, a radioactive cloud was already spreading far and wide. Later reactors included built-in safety measures in order to prevent such problems from happening again.

CASE STUDY

Three Mile Island

In 1979, the U.S. nuclear power programme suffered a serious setback. The Three Mile Island power station in Pennsylvania had two pressurized water reactors. An accident in one of them happened due to a fault in the cooling system. The reactor automatically shut down in about one second, but it was too late. A relief valve failed to close and more than a third of the fuel melted. Problems with instruments in the control room were partly to blame for the damage that this caused. Radiation was released and the public feared the worst. Even though serious injury and contamination were avoided, public confidence in nuclear energy was damaged. It led to a decline in U.S. nuclear station construction throughout the 1980s and 1990s. However, many safety lessons were learned and, today, the USA has over 100 nuclear reactors with a reputed high level of safety, providing almost 20 percent of its electricity.

The release of radiation from the Three Mile Island nuclear power station put serious doubts into people's minds as to how safe these plants are.

Dangers

Nuclear power stations, like the one at Three Mile Island (page 17), must be built near to the sea or rivers, as they need a lot of water for cooling. One of the greatest dangers to a power station is if it overheats. That's what happened in the disaster at Chernobyl in the former USSR (now Ukraine). It was the worst nuclear power accident in history.

In April 1986, an experiment at the Chernobyl power station caused the reactor core to overheat and melt. The reactor's lid was blown off, and large amounts of radioactive material were released into the atmosphere. The explosion killed 32 people immediately and 130,000 people had to be evacuated. The radioactive cloud that blew over Europe caused many casualties over a long period.

CASE STUDY

Contamination

Twenty years after the Chernobyl disaster, two scientists studied the birdlife around Chernobyl to see the impact it had on local wildlife. Timothy Mousseau and Anders Moller carried out a census at different sites, recording 57 species, before comparing their findings with local radiation levels. They found that the higher the level of radiation, the lower the number of birds. Their findings suggested that birds were still affected by the loss of their main source of food in contaminated soil. This study on radiation levels, bird numbers, body mass, egg size, and bird migration distances also showed that brightly coloured bird species were worst affected. Such species rely on important chemicals in their food called **antioxidants** to colour their feathers or beaks. The scientists think that levels of naturally occurring antioxidants must have been affected, too.

A helicopter uses water in an attempt to cool down Chernobyl's destroyed reactor hall.

Ukraine's health ministry estimated that 15,000 people died and 3.5 million people suffered illness as a result of the contamination. Exact numbers are uncertain, but ever since the accident there has been much international concern over the safety of nuclear energy.

Natural dangers

It isn't just human error that threatens the safety of nuclear power stations. In July 2007, a Japanese power plant had to shut down after an earthquake. The nuclear plant, near the city of Kashiwazaki, was shaken so much that 100 drums of radioactive waste fell over. Some of the lids opened and the contents spilled out.

CUTTING EDGE: BEING A SAFE PLANT

Japan relies on 55 nuclear reactors for about a third of its electricity. Being prone to earthquakes, Japan has strict regulations to prevent damage to its nuclear plants. They include building nuclear plants on solid **bedrock** to limit shaking from earthquakes and building anti-**tsunami** walls at plants along the coast, like at Kashiwazaki. Even so, the 2007 earthquake still gave the Kashiwazaki plant a serious shake-up!

Emergency crews at Kashiwazaki nuclear plant assess the damage after the 2007 earthquake.

21st century power

Despite concerns in the 1990s, with some countries halting their nuclear power programmes altogether, the 21st century has seen a renewed enthusiasm for nuclear development. With many countries now committed to cutting carbon emissions over the next decade in order to reduce their effect on global warming, one of the solutions is to build more nuclear power plants. This is because they produce hardly any carbon dioxide. Nuclear power is said to save the planet from two billion tonnes of carbon dioxide every year, which would otherwise be produced by coal-fired power stations. Even so, nuclear power still provides less than 20 percent of the world's electricity.

Nuclear research is continuing to improve the efficiency of reactors. Scientists around the world keep testing ideas, using the results and evidence to improve methods and designs, while constantly developing nuclear technology. With the working life of most nuclear reactors being between 30 and 40 years, scientists are investigating how to extend it in the future.

The two generating units of China's Tianwan nuclear power plant, built as a joint project between China and Russia.

Nuclear development

Today, the world produces as much electricity from nuclear energy as it did from all sources combined in 1960. Nuclear energy accounts for 16 percent of the electricity generated in the world today. The following are just some of the main countries involved in nuclear power development programmes:

- China has 11 nuclear power reactors in commercial operation, 6 under construction, and several more about to start construction.
- France produces over 75 percent of its electricity from nuclear energy and even exports electricity.
- India aims to supply 25 percent of its electricity from nuclear power by 2050.
- Japan's 55 reactors provide 30 percent of the country's electricity.
- The UK has 19 reactors, generating 20 percent of its electricity, but 18 will be retired by 2023. The next generation of plants won't open until 2017.
- The USA has over 100 nuclear power reactors, providing almost 20 percent of its electricity. New nuclear capacity is expected by 2020.
- Australia has no nuclear power, but supplies 24 percent of world uranium.

Although the world's energy needs will continue to grow, it is still expected that most of the demand will be met by burning **fossil fuels**.

The growing consumption of energy across the world can clearly be seen in this graph, with its projections for future consumption rates. Although much of this energy is used to generate electricity, a large proportion of the oil consumed is for other purposes.

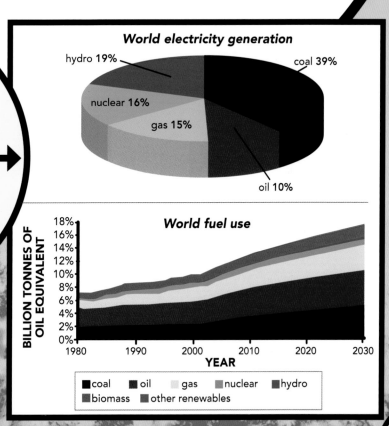

World electricity generation

hydro 19%
coal 39%
nuclear 16%
gas 15%
oil 10%

World fuel use

BILLION TONNES OF OIL EQUIVALENT

coal · oil · gas · nuclear · hydro
biomass · other renewables

Driving force

As well as the 30 countries running commercial nuclear power reactors, there are 56 countries operating nearly 300 nuclear reactors for research, and a further 220 reactors that power ships and submarines.

Submarines

Nuclear submarines are among the most powerful vessels to have been invented. The first one was commissioned in 1954 – the USS *Nautilus*. For the first time, a submarine could go twice around the world, underwater, without the need to refuel. Nuclear submarines, ships, and rockets use energy released by a nuclear reaction to provide thrust. This is known as nuclear **propulsion**. As nuclear reactors don't need air or oxygen, nuclear propulsion allows a submarine to stay underwater for a very long time.

This U.S. navy aircraft carrier, the USS *George Washington*, is nuclear powered.

 THE SCIENCE YOU LEARN: ENERGY TRANSFORMATION

Energy transformation is the process of changing one form of energy into another. The energy of fossil fuels, moving water, sunlight, or nuclear fuel can be converted into other forms, such as heating, electricity, and movement. A nuclear-powered ship or submarine uses a nuclear reactor to generate heat. The heat comes from nuclear fuel contained within the reactor. The nuclear fuel contains more than one million times as much energy per unit mass as chemical fuel. The heat produced in the reactor is used to create steam. The steam is used to drive the main propulsion turbines, which drive the propeller. The steam also drives the generators that supply the ship with electricity.

The USA, UK, Russia, and France have nuclear submarines. There are two types of nuclear submarine. Attack submarines – like the USS *Seawolf* – weigh about 9,000 tonnes and carry torpedoes to fire against enemy ships and submarines. Ballistic missile submarines – like the USS *Ohio* – are much bigger. Weighing about 19,000 tonnes, they can launch missiles against enemy land targets thousands of miles away.

For the record

Plutonium has powered 24 U.S. space vehicles. It provided the power for the two Voyager spacecraft, which sent back important pictures of distant planets. These spacecraft, launched in 1977, have operated for over 30 years and may continue to do so for another 20. The Cassini spacecraft, launched in 1997, carries three generators to provide power as it orbits Saturn.

This is a model of the Ford Nucleon, designed in 1958. This car was to be nuclear-powered, but none were actually built!

CUTTING EDGE: ROCKETS TO MARS!

NASA scientists are now working on nuclear-propelled rockets to take people to the Moon, Mars, and beyond. Dr. Gerald Smith of Positronics Research said: *"The current reference mission calls for a nuclear reactor to propel the spaceship to Mars. This is desirable because nuclear propulsion reduces travel time to Mars, increasing safety for the crew by reducing their exposure to **cosmic rays**. Also, a chemically-powered spacecraft weighs much more and costs a lot more to launch. The reactor also provides ample power for the three-year mission. But nuclear reactors are complex, so more things could potentially go wrong during the mission."*

Radiation risks

Uranium and plutonium are not the only unstable isotopes that cause radioactive decay. Other isotopes also release high-energy particles or waves that cause ionizing radiation, which can be harmful to living things, including humans. There are three kinds of ionizing radiation and each can damage or destroy living cells.

Alpha, beta, gamma

Alpha particles have a large electrical charge and can ionize other atoms. Alpha particles, as given off by some uranium atoms, are heavy and move slowly over a short range in air, and can be stopped by something as thin as a sheet of paper. Even though alpha particles cannot penetrate your skin, it is possible to eat or drink something contaminated with them. Once inside you, they could ionize atoms in your body cells, which may cause cells to become cancerous.

Beta particles are fast and light. They ionize atoms that they pass but not as strongly as alpha particles. However, they can get through your skin and affect cells inside you.

Gamma rays are electromagnetic waves with no mass (so they are not particles), like X-rays. Gamma rays hardly ionize atoms at all, so they do not cause damage directly. However, gamma rays are very difficult to stop and only lead or concrete can shield you from them. When gamma rays enter an atom, they can make that atom emit other particles. If that atom is in one of your body cells this process could be harmful.

After the Chernobyl disaster (see page 18), many people were exposed to **radioactivity** around the burning power station. It is now believed that this has led to a massive increase of cancer in the regions around Chernobyl. Scientists estimate that people living in contaminated areas are twice as likely to suffer from disease as people living in clean areas.

Health and safety

With so much energy from atomic nuclei buzzing all around us, are we really safe, and what harm can they do? The risk of our body cells being affected by radioactivity is very small. Only high or prolonged doses of radioactivity cause damage to our bodies and become life threatening.

Radiation sickness

Sometimes radioactive particles pass right through our bodies with no effect, but there are other times when they affect our **DNA**. Damage can occur when DNA is exposed to radioactive particles. Radiation can cause the body's atoms to become electrically charged, which can lead to radiation sickness and different types of cancer. High doses of radioactivity can kill a human within 24 hours.

Because all uranium isotopes are alpha emitters, they are only harmful if breathed in or swallowed. However, some uranium emits gamma rays, so people who work with or near large quantities of uranium can be exposed to harmful radiation. Radiation can damage the **immune system** and tissues of the body. Among the body's cells that are most sensitive to radiation are the red blood cells and the white blood cells that fight infection.

The first organ affected after exposure to high radiation is the stomach (shown here as dark pink, with a glowing sphere), causing vomiting. Next are the intestines (centre bottom), causing diarrhoea. The bone marrow is also affected, leading to a reduction in blood cells. Damage to blood vessels in the liver (centre left), and kidneys, leads to the build up of toxic substances in the blood. Inflammation of the lungs (light pink) causes breathing problems. Cases in which all these symptoms appear generally prove fatal (result in death) within one week.

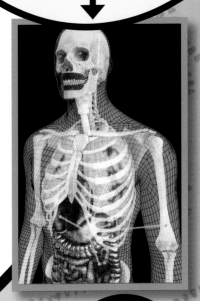

CASE STUDY

Alexander Litvinenko

In 2006, former Russian spy Alexander Litvinenko fell ill after eating a sushi dinner. He was taken to a London hospital where he later died of radiation sickness. He accused a Russian of poisoning his food. Polonium, a radioactive element found in uranium ores (polonium-210), was discovered inside his body. Doctors were unable to save him from the fatal effects of radiation.

Radioactivity around us

We are all exposed to low levels of radiation all the time. For example, **radon** gas can be found anywhere. Other sources are: food and drink, the ground, and cosmic rays, such as gamma rays. Hardly any background radiation comes from nuclear reactors or nuclear waste. In fact, you are more likely to be exposed to radiation if you fly in a plane, as there are more cosmic rays higher in the atmosphere. So how much radiation does the average person receive each year? The investigation on the right will give you an idea.

Marie Curie

Marie Curie was one of the first female scientists to become accepted by her peers. She won two Nobel Prizes and her work led to a far greater understanding of radioactivity. However, it came at a cost to her health – she died from cancer as a result of her long exposure to radioactive particles. Her notebooks are still radioactive! By 1896, Antoine Becquerel had discovered that uranium was radioactive. This was of great interest to Curie and her husband, Pierre, who were studying the properties of different elements. Because of their work, we now know that, apart from uranium, there are eight other naturally radioactive elements: polonium, astatine, radon, francium, actinium, thorium, protactinium, and **radium**. We also know that human-made elements heavier than uranium, like plutonium, are also radioactive. Curie found radium to be 2 million times more radioactive than uranium. When radium decays, it produces a radioactive gas called radon, which is present wherever uranium is found. In some parts of the world this gas seeps out of soils containing uranium and may sometimes accumulate inside buildings. People who live and work in such buildings could be exposed to unhealthy levels of radioactivity.

THE SCIENCE YOU LEARN: MILLIREMS

A unit of radiation dose is measured in millirems. On average, people in Western countries receive a dose of about 300 millirems each year from natural background radiation. It is believed that even 5,000–10,000 millirems received in a short time, or over a long period, can be safe with no observable health effects.

INVESTIGATION: CALCULATING YOUR PERSONAL LEVELS OF RADIATION

Add up your score as you work through these questions to get your personal levels of radiation per year. Results are approximate and given in millirems.

Where you live
1. Cosmic radiation at sea level (from outer space)   **+ 26**

2. Select the number of millirems for your elevation (in feet)

up to 1,000 ft. = 2	3,000–4,000 ft. = 9	7,000–8,000 ft. = 53
1,000–2,000 ft. = 5	4,000–5,000 ft. = 21	8,000–9,000 ft. = 70
2,000–3,000 ft. = 9	5,000–6,000 ft. = 29	
3,000–4,000 ft. = 9	6,000–7,000 ft. = 40	add this number: +_____

3. Terrestrial (from the ground): this varies according to rocks, soils, etc.,
but an average would be about   **+ 55**

4. House construction: if you live in a stone, brick, or concrete building, add 7   +_____

What you eat and drink
5. From food and water   **+ 40**

From air (radon)   **+ 200**

Other sources
6. Weapons test fallout   **+ 1**

7. Jet plane travel: for each 1,000 miles you have travelled, add 1   +_____

8. If you wear a luminous (LCD) wristwatch, add 0.006   +_____

9. If you have used luggage inspection at airports
(using a typical X-ray machine), add 0.002   +_____

10. If you watch TV, add 1   +_____

11. If you use a video display terminal (VDT), add 1   +_____

12. If you have a smoke detector, add 0.008   +_____

13. If you have had medical X-rays in the last year, add 40   +_____

14. If you live within 50 miles of a nuclear power plant, add 0.0009   +_____

15. If you live within 50 miles of a coal-fired electrical utility plant, add 0.03   +_____

Total annual millirems dose: _____

You can also calculate your dose on-line at
http://www.nrc.gov/about-nrc/radiation/around-us/calculator.html

Am I safe?
Don't worry – your total score is healthy, even if you work in a nuclear power station every day of the year! The normal levels of background radiation are harmless.

Radiation detection

The problem with radioactive materials, such as alpha particles, beta particles, or gamma rays, is that they are totally invisible. So how can we tell where they are and what level of radiation exists? This was the question facing a German scientist 100 years ago.

From 1906–1912, Hans Wilhelm Geiger worked on radioactivity in Manchester, England, with Ernest Rutherford (see page 4). In 1908, he designed an instrument to detect and count alpha particles. Then he worked with another scientist, Walther Müller, and developed the Geiger-Müller counter – an instrument that detects all forms of ionizing radiation. Such radiation includes alpha and beta particles, as well as gamma rays. Today, scientists use Geiger counters to find uranium and other radioactive elements, as well as detect levels of contamination on clothes or in the atmosphere. Many modern Geiger counters still use the same basic design as the first model, although more advanced detectors are also in use.

This scientist is using a Geiger counter to detect radiation in the environment.

Small Geiger counters can only provide limited information and struggle to detect very weak radiation fields. But cutting edge science is providing answers. Brad Jones, a professor of chemistry at Wake Forest University in the USA, is leading research to develop the first handheld instrument capable of detecting and identifying radioactive particles in detail outside the laboratory. Linked to a laptop computer, the results are instantly analyzed in detail and display each sample's wavelength and intensity on a graph. This allows scientists to identify specific elements and precise amounts of radioactivity.

According to Professor Jones: *"The proposed device represents a new way of thinking in the field of nuclear forensics. Atomic emission **spectrometry** is traditionally a laboratory-based technique using very large, very expensive instruments. With immediate on-site results, residents could be given information about a potential threat, or reassured that none existed, rather than waiting for samples to be transported to laboratories for analysis".*

Jones and his team of scientists hope to develop the new type of Geiger counter by 2010.

The electromagnetic spectrum diagram

low frequency

KHz	10	extremely low frequency (ELF)
	10^2	
	10^4	very low frequency (VLF)
MHz	10^6	
non-ionizing radiation	10^8	radio waves, mobile phone
GHz		microwaves
	10^{10}	
	10^{12}	infrared radiation
	10^{14}	visible light
	10^{16}	ultraviolet radiation
ionizing radiation	10^{18}	X-rays
	10^{20}	
	10^{22}	gamma rays
	10^{24}	
	10^{26}	

high frequency

Detecting risky phones

Geiger counters have been used to test mobile phones that emit a small amount of electromagnetic radiation. Scientists have tried to find out whether radiation from phones damages the tissue inside our heads during calls. Electromagnetic radiation is made up of waves of electric and magnetic energy moving at the speed of light. It ranges from extremely low frequency radiation to more harmful X-rays and gamma rays. The diagram shows the two types of electromagnetic radiation:

- Ionizing radiation, which contains enough electromagnetic energy to damage atoms in our bodies and alter chemical reactions inside us. Gamma rays and X-rays are two forms of ionizing radiation.
- Non-ionizing radiation, which is usually safe. It generates heat, but not usually enough to cause any long-term damage to body tissue.

THE SCIENCE YOU LEARN: MEASURING RADIOACTIVITY

The amount of radiation being given off by radioactive material is measured using the unit curie (Ci), named after the scientist Marie Curie (see page 26). A curie is a unit of radioactivity, whereas a millirem (see page 26) is a unit of radiation dose.

CASE STUDY

Are power lines, mobile phones, and radio masts safe?

In August 2007, an international group of scientists and researchers (The BioInitiative Working Group) released a report on electromagnetic fields (EMF) and health. They reported serious scientific concerns about current limits regulating how much EMF is allowable from power lines, mobile phones, and many other sources of EMF exposure in daily life. The report stated that existing standards for public safety are inadequate to protect public health. More work is still to be done in order to find out the effects of electromagnetic waves on our health.

Lasting effects

Another problem with radioactive material is the long time it takes for its harmful effects to become safe. Different isotopes vary in the number of years they take to change and become non-radioactive.

Radioactive dating

Even though radioactivity is generally thought of as harmful, it does have its uses to scientists and those studying ancient remains. By knowing the half-life of a radioactive element (see panel below), it is possible to work out its age by studying the amount of decay. By using this radioactive dating, which measures the amount of radioactive material (usually carbon-14) that an object contains, scientists can determine the age of an ancient object, such as a fossil. Animals and plants have a small amount of carbon-14 in their tissues (as well as carbon-12) and, after their death, the amount of carbon-14 in their remains disintegrates at a known rate (carbon-14 has a half-life of 5,700 years). Scientists just have to measure the amount of carbon-14 that is left to work out the age of the remains.

A large dinosaur skeleton is carefully removed from the ground before it is accurately dated using nuclear technology.

Radioactive dating relies on the properties of isotopes (like those of carbon or uranium) that are identical except for the number of neutrons in their nucleus. Being unstable, such isotopes shed particles until the nucleus becomes stable. The result is like a radioactive clock that ticks away, with unstable isotopes decaying into stable ones. To read the time on this radioactive clock, scientists use a device called a **mass spectrometer.**

THE SCIENCE YOU LEARN:
MEASURING RADIOACTIVE DECAY

Scientists measure radioactivity decay in units of time called half-lives. The half-life is the time it takes for a radioactive material to decay to one half of its original amount, which is when one half of the atoms have disintegrated. Half-lives can vary from millionths of a second to billions of years. All isotopes of uranium and plutonium are radioactive, with most having extremely long half-lives.

Isotopes and their half-lives

Isotope	Half-life
Uranium-234 (U-234)	245,000 years
Uranium-235 (U-235)	704 million years
Uranium-238 (U-238)	4.46 billion years
Plutonium-238 (Pu-238)	88 years
Plutonium-241 (Pu-241)	14.3 years
Plutonium-242 (Pu-242)	376,000 years
Plutonium-244 (Pu-244) (occurs naturally)	80 million years
Carbon-14 (C-14)	5,700 years
Strontium-90 (Sr-90)	28 years
Polonium-210 (Po-210)	138 days
Radon-222 (Rn-222)	4 days

This table shows the half-lives of some radioactive isotopes. We can see that the length of time it takes for half of their atoms to change composition varies greatly, from days to billions of years!

This scientist is using a mass spectrometer in a laboratory to measure carbon dating.

CUTTING EDGE: UNLOCKING THE PAST

If scientists are trying to date bones from millions of years ago, radiocarbon dating cannot be used because the short half-life of carbon-14 isotopes won't work on bones over 50,000 years old. Instead, for really old fossils, scientists need an isotope with a very long half-life. One of the isotopes used for this purpose is Uranium-235 (U-235), which has a half-life of over 700 million years. However, bones do not contain uranium, so scientists have to measure rocks surrounding the fossils or nearby volcanic ash to work out when the bones were deposited. In this way, nuclear physics is able to help us understand some of the ancient mysteries of our planet.

Making waste safe

If radioactive material remains dangerous for so long, what can be done to make nuclear waste safe? The leftover isotopes from nuclear reactors can be highly radioactive for thousands of years, so the big problem for scientists is working out how to dispose of radioactive material without endangering future generations. The U.S. National Academy of Sciences reports that it will take 3 million years for some radioactive waste to decay to safe levels. The only solution so far has been to store the waste out of the way where it stays safe.

High-level waste consists mainly of spent nuclear reactor fuel. Nuclear power plants in the USA alone produce 3,000 tons of high-level waste each year. The amount of spent fuel removed each year in the USA would fill a football field to a depth of one foot. If the UK's reactors keep working as long as expected, there will be about 36,590 cubic metres of high-level waste – enough to fill 14 Olympic-sized swimming pools. Most of the UK's low-level waste is stored in sealed concrete vaults. The Drigg store in Cumbria, UK, currently holds the equivalent to 384 Olympic swimming pools worth of low-level waste. Lower level radioactive waste includes:

- protective clothing worn by workers in contact with radioactive materials
- cooling water, used fuel rods, old tools, and disused parts from nuclear power plants
- **mill tailings** from uranium-enrichment factories
- old medical radiation equipment from hospitals and clinics
- used smoke detectors that contain radioactive material.

Here, radioactive spent fuel rods are stored in pools of water with lead-lined concrete walls.

Storage problems

Nuclear power plants usually store their spent fuel rods in pools of water with lead-lined concrete walls to contain the spread of gamma radiation. For long-term storage of high-level waste, the problem for scientists is designing leak-proof containers and building deep bunkers that are safe from earthquakes.

One technique for packaging high-level waste involves melting it with glass and pouring the **molten** material into containers. The containers are then buried. Some scientists and environmentalists question if these buried containers will survive the tens of thousands of years it takes for this high-level waste to decay to safe levels.

Barrels of radioactive waste were sometimes dumped in oceans. This was until 1970, when the Environmental Protection Agency (EPA) realized that 25 percent of these barrels were leaking. Scientists today are working on safer ways to deal with the radioactive waste left after nuclear fission.

Handling radioactive waste safely is very important.

CUTTING EDGE:
REMOVING STRONTIUM FROM LIQUID NUCLEAR WASTE

A team of scientists at Northwestern University, USA., is working on a new way to remove the radioactive material strontium from liquid nuclear waste. Nuclear reactors produce large amounts of radioactive liquid that has to be stored in massive tanks. Strontium-90 is one of the most dangerous radioactive materials in this waste. But the latest project uses chemicals to filter out the strontium as a solid material, leaving clean liquid behind. The radioactive solid could then be stored or recycled and the liquid disposed of safely. This is just one attempt by scientists to try to deal with those deadly tanks of toxic, nuclear sludge.

Source: http://www.sciencedaily.com/releases/2008/03/080303190649.htm

Useful radiation

Despite the health dangers from radioactive particles and rays, the energy released from the nuclei of many atoms can be lifesaving. Radiation and nuclear medicine are used to treat many patients in modern hospitals. Gamma rays are used for sterilizing hospital equipment and bandages. This is especially useful for killing bacteria on plastic syringes that would be damaged if heated. X-rays are also used to help doctors diagnose all kinds of medical conditions.

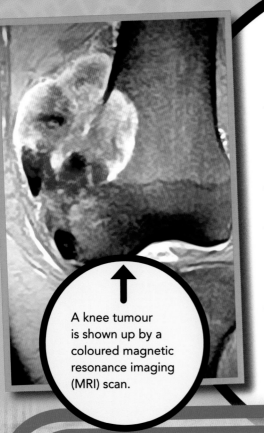

A knee tumour is shown up by a coloured magnetic resonance imaging (MRI) scan.

X-rays and saving lives

Since the German scientist Wilhelm Röntgen made a discovery in 1895 while experimenting with electron beams, doctors have used X-rays to see inside patients' bodies. In fact, in the early days of X-ray science, doctors would often expose patients to the beams for long periods. Because of this, some doctors and patients started to develop radiation sickness, because X-rays are a form of ionizing radiation.

Ions

When normal light hits an atom, it doesn't change the atom at all. When an X-ray hits an atom, it can knock electrons from the atom to create an **ion**. Free electrons then collide with other atoms to create more ions. As scientists now know, an ion's electrical charge can lead to reactions inside atoms of the body. X-rays are valuable tools in hospitals and are far safer today than they were in Röntgen's day (see above). However, because of the risks associated with them, they are now used less often.

Chemical tracers

Another way nuclear science helps patients today is with radioactive chemicals called tracers. Certain chemicals collect at damaged or diseased parts of the body, and the radioactive tracers accumulate with them. Radiation detectors placed outside the body detect the radiation emitted and, with the aid of computers, build up an image of the inside of the body. The radioactive chemical has to have a short half-life so that it stops working before it can do any damage.

Tracers giving off beta or gamma radiation are used because these types of radiation pass out of the body and are less likely to be absorbed by cells than alpha radiation. Such tracers are even used on the heart to allow cameras outside of the body to read the energy and create pictures of different parts of the heart. Such radiation imaging is known as **radiology**, but it is with the science of radiotherapy that many hospital patients might be more familiar.

A radioactive tracer that attaches itself to diseased cells is injected into a patient. The white and blue areas are those with a high concentration of those cells.

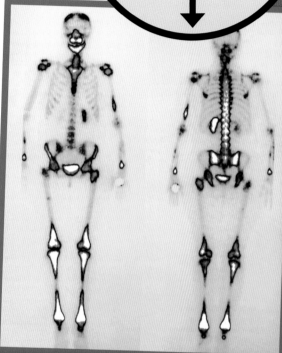

CUTTING EDGE: MRI SCANNING

New technology allows detailed internal images to be taken without using X-rays or other ionizing radiation. This is done with Magnetic Resonance Imaging (MRI) scans. An MRI scan is able to show fine detail of different organs and tissues by reading the hydrogen atoms in the body. Hydrogen atoms are just right for MRI because their nuclei have a single proton, and when placed in a magnetic field the hydrogen atoms line up and can be analyzed by a scanner. The machine reads the information inside a patient's hydrogen protons and creates safe, detailed pictures.

This nuclear imaging is useful for detecting:
- **tumours**
- weak areas in blood vessels
- blood cell disorders and blood flow problems.

Radiotherapy

Although radiation can cause cancer, it can also help to treat disease. Doctors have learned how to use radioactivity to stop cancer spreading. Since scientists discovered that some levels of radioactivity kill body cells, doctors have been able to target areas of cancer with radioactivity to stop the cancer cells from growing or multiplying.

Cancer cells usually multiply faster than other cells in the body. Because radiation is most harmful to rapidly growing cells, radiation therapy damages cancerous cells more than normal cells. Ionizing radiation can penetrate tissue and alter the part of the cell that regulates its growth and reproduction. Healthy cells can recover from this damage, but cancerous cells cannot.

CASE STUDY

Gamma knife radiotherapy is usually used to treat brain tumours. The frame prevents the head from moving during treatment.

Gamma knife radiotherapy

For a brain tumour, the patient receives a low gamma radiation dose given through a helmet. It is targeted at a specific region of the brain to avoid affecting surrounding tissue. This type of radiotherapy provides access to areas of the brain that cannot otherwise be reached.

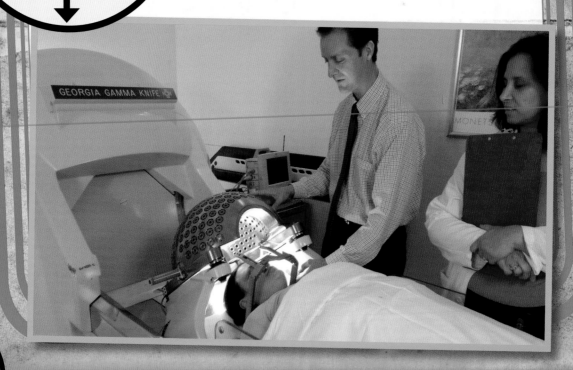

However, this process can sometimes kill healthy cells, so patients may develop side effects during treatment, depending on the dose or part of the body receiving radiation. Some of the more common side effects are hair loss, skin discomfort, tiredness, and other symptoms of radiation sickness.

Radiation can prevent cancer from coming back after a tumour has been removed by surgery. There are two types of radiation therapy:

- external beam radiation is most frequently used. This uses an X-ray machine to aim high-powered rays directly at the tumour from outside of the body.
- internal beam radiation uses radioactive implants placed directly into or near the tumour.

This patient is receiving radiotherapy. The pattern alignment shows where radiation will be applied.

Progress

Researchers are working to improve radiotherapy by targeting beams of nuclear energy more precisely, as well as making the cancer cells more sensitive to it by using various chemicals. As modern radiotherapy equipment targets tumours more precisely, smaller doses are required, which in turn lessen the risk to healthy body cells. In recent years, with advances in both radiology as well as radiotherapy, cancer patients have a far better chance of survival than in the past. Scientists researching nuclear medicine continue to make important progress.

Radiation at work

Not only are radioactive rays used in medicine, they are also used in many industries. As technology continues to develop, radiation can be used safely for more and more tasks.

X-rays at work

Baggage handlers use X-rays on airport luggage for security. But X-rays are also often used in the building industry. They can reveal structural information that could be missed by the human eye, such as cracks in metal girders. X-rays are also used to reveal stress-related changes in bridges, road surfaces, and even aircraft.

Seeing below the surface

Just as radiation machines use radioactive tracer chemicals in the human body to read hidden information, engineers use similar technology to find cracked pipes underground. By pumping radioactive tracer chemicals through the pipes, engineers can use a scanner above ground to create images of what is happening underground. In this way, environmental scientists and engineers can monitor underground drainage to measure pollution discharges from factories and sewage plants. Scanners using radiation can also be used in the sea to measure pollution, the movement of silt (fine sand or clay deposits), or to provide images of underwater pipelines. Radioactive materials used for such purposes have short half-lives and decay to background levels within days.

At airports, X-rays are used to show security personnel exactly what you have in your luggage.

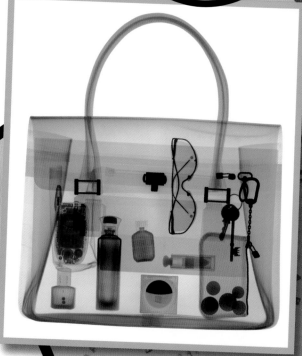

THE SCIENCE IN THE HOME: RADIOACTIVE DEVICES

Many homes contain a variety of relatively harmless radioactive devices; from clocks or watches that glow in the dark to lifesaving smoke alarms. Smoke detectors use a small amount of radiation to sense smoke. Just a small amount of smoke creates a current in the detector, which triggers a loud alarm. Such devices save lives in homes around the world. Can you find any radioactive devices in your home?

Rays for measurement

Many industries require precise measuring and monitoring of very thin materials. Radiation is often used to control the thickness of materials such as paper, plastic, and aluminium. Thicker material absorbs more radiation, so less radiation reaches the detector. Signals from the detector can be used to adjust equipment that controls the thickness of the material, ensuring that it is made to the exact requirements.

Smoke detectors

Inside every smoke detector is a small amount of a radioactive element that releases alpha particles (generally as little as 1/5000th of a gram with a half-life of 432 years). The average smoke detector contains just 0.9 microcuries of americium-241.

One curie (see page 29) undergoes 37 billion nuclear transformations per second. This means that 37 billion atoms in the material are decaying and emitting an alpha particle of nuclear radiation per second.

Although smoke detectors are safe, you should never open up the internal workings of one – the alpha particles might become airborne and could be breathed in.

A smoke detector holds a radioactive isotope, e.g. americium-241. Any smoke entering the small chamber is ionized by the radiation and conducts a current, setting off an alarm.

Fusion

As well as splitting certain atoms to release nuclear energy by fission, scientists discovered another way atoms can be used to create immense power. It involves joining atoms together, and is known as **nuclear fusion**.

Joining together

Scientists have long argued about how stars in the sky created their energy. In 1939, the German-born scientist Hans Bethe proposed that the energy produced by the Sun is created by the fusion of hydrogen nuclei into helium. He went on to win the Nobel Prize for his discoveries about the energy of stars. But it was while he was working on the first atom bomb that he developed the idea of fusing atoms to make energy on Earth.

CASE STUDY

Bethe and the hydrogen bomb

During the early 1950s, scientist Hans Bethe joined a project to make a hydrogen bomb. He hoped to prove it couldn't be made. However, it was built, and the first nuclear fusion bomb was tested in 1952. Two years later, on 1st March 1954, the U.S. tested a hydrogen bomb on the island of Bikini in the Pacific Ocean. The energy it released shocked even the scientists and it remains the biggest thermonuclear hydrogen bomb detonated to this day. It was 1,000 times more powerful than the bomb dropped on Hiroshima during World War II (see page 10):

"I was on a ship that was 30 miles away, and we had this horrible white stuff raining down on us. I got 10 rads of radiation from it. It was pretty frightening. There was a huge fireball with these turbulent rolls going in and out. The thing was glowing... It spread until the edge of it looked as if it was almost directly overhead. It was a much more awesome sight than a puny little atomic bomb. It was a pretty sobering and shattering experience."

Eyewitness U.S. physicist Marshall Rosenbluth

Two nuclei, here deuterium and tritium, fuse together to form a new element (helium), a fast-moving neutron, and a large amount of energy. Fusion reactors use deuterium and tritium for fuel because they will fuse at a lower temperature. Deuterium can be easily extracted from seawater so the fuel is cheap and plentiful.

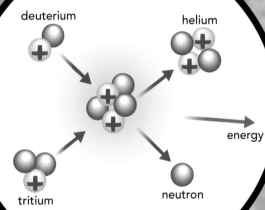

deuterium

helium

energy

tritium

neutron

Nuclear fusion powers the Sun, and affects all life on Earth.

The physics involved

Fusion is what happens when two atomic nuclei are forced together by high pressure to make a large nucleus. There has to be high pressure to overcome the strong resisting force in the nuclei. The pressure to set off the fusion reaction over 50 years ago at Bikini was supplied by the energy of an atomic bomb, and the fusion reaction that resulted was called the H Bomb. Scientists have been trying to control nuclear fusion ever since. Various fusion reactors have attempted to produce electricity but they have had trouble controlling the reaction in a contained space. Nuclear fusion creates less radioactive material than fission. The hope is that one day the benefits will make the investment of resources in research and development worthwhile.

The big question

If the Sun uses nuclear fusion of hydrogen atoms into helium atoms to give off heat and light, why can't we build a machine to do the same? Even though no sustained reaction has yet been achieved for fusion, it could be just a matter of time now…

Energy like never before

In theory, it should be possible to fuse atoms, release neutrons, and generate cheap renewable energy. One kilogram of fusion fuel would produce the same amount of energy as 10 million kilograms of fossil fuel. Fusion power stations, as with fission reactors, would use escaping neutrons to heat water into steam that drives turbines, which would – in turn – generate energy. Fusion would still create radioactive waste but not the amount of long-term, high-level radioactive material that is produced by nuclear fission. It would actually make less radiation than the natural background radiation we live with in our daily lives. Radioactive material created from fusion decays rapidly and the time before it could be handled can be reduced to about 50 years. One of the main fusion by-products is helium – a harmless gas. So, fusion reactors could be a very clean technology. Even if the **plasma** escapes, it immediately cools and the reaction stops. Fusion seems the answer to all our problems.

So if that's the theory, why doesn't it happen? Unfortunately, there's a catch. Turning the calculations into reality is easier said than done, because it all depends on extreme temperatures. After all, fusion does occur naturally, but not on Earth – it happens in the Sun. The energy to force nuclei together comes from the intense, internal temperatures of the Sun, approaching 20 million°C (36 million°F) or more at the centre! So forcing nuclei to fuse on Earth means heating them to extremes.

One way of doing this is to cause the nuclei to move so fast that they generate the immense heat required. But then the great task would be to control and contain the reaction. To some, this might seem like an impossible task. However, scientists are confident that they can develop the technology to do this, and their success could only be a matter of years away.

False hopes?

In 1989, two scientists at the University of Utah, USA, claimed to have produced nuclear fusion at room temperature, creating great heat but no radiation. The world of science was astounded by such claims and other scientists tried to repeat the process. Sadly, it did not work and the research of what is now called cold fusion was set back many years. However, in 2005, cold fusion got another boost when scientists made further progress with research at room temperature.

In 1989, Stanley Pons (right) and Martin Fleischmann (left) claimed to have discovered cold fusion. This caused a storm in the science world but proved to be short-lived as the process failed.

THE SCIENCE YOU LEARN: SCIENTIFIC METHOD

Scientists must keep to strict rules and follow a set scientific method. Only then can the science be tested and proved – with hard evidence. The key parts involved in scientific method are:

- Developing an **hypothesis** by careful observation. In physics, the hypothesis often takes the form of a mathematical equation.
- Using the hypothesis to predict outcomes, the existence of other phenomena, and the results of new observations.
- Performing thorough experimental tests, recording outcomes accurately, and using independent experimenters to observe and analyze the process.

Learning from mistakes

The cold fusion scientists made fundamental mistakes that could easily have been avoided by following the correct scientific method.

"Although cold fusion is considered controversial, the scientific process demands of us to keep an open mind and examine the new results once every few years", said Gopal Coimbatore of the American Chemical Society's Division of Environmental Chemistry.

In fact, some researchers now believe they have new evidence that cold fusion, now called low energy nuclear reactions, has developed further and is making progress. So, listen out for news!

Scientists on the brink

The biggest research project into nuclear fusion involves hundreds of scientists from all around the world. This is huge physics, like never before – it's equivalent to building a star on Earth!

The groundwork

A fusion test reactor at the Princeton Plasma Physics Laboratory, USA, set world records from 1982 to 1997. It produced temperatures of 510 million°C (918 million°F) – the highest ever produced in a laboratory, and well beyond the 100 million°C (180 million°F) required for commercial fusion. In 1994, the reactor produced a world-record 10.7 million watts of controlled fusion power, enough to meet the needs of more than 3,000 homes.

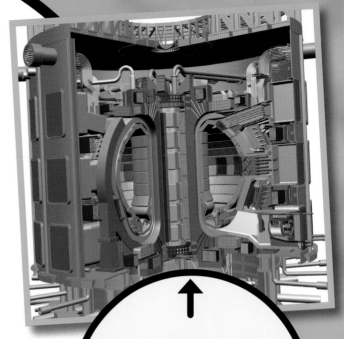

The huge ITER reactor is being built in France. It is based on a Russian design called a **tokamak**, in which gas is heated to over 100 million°C (180 million°F) in order to produce fusion power.

Important steps

Scientists at the Joint European Torus (JET) fusion reactor at Culham, UK, made important progress in 1997 when they produced a record output of energy. However, the energy was not maintained for long and it took about 50 percent more energy to produce than it created. Even so, this was an important step in developing fusion research.

CUTTING EDGE: THE LEAP FORWARD

The International Thermonuclear Experimental Reactor (ITER) may be able to solve the problems of fusion. The U.S., Europe, Russia, India, China, Korea, and Japan are building this giant project at Cadarache, in the South of France. The ITER project will cost billions. The hope is that it will eventually produce the first fusion reactor to produce more energy than it consumes. ITER is predicted to be the reactor that sparks all of humankind to use the power of the stars! The design phase was finished in 2001 and the first work with plasmas is forecast for 2016. The operating phase should last at least 20 years.

Is ITER worth it?

ITER will be the first full-scale fusion device to produce energy at the level of an electricity-producing power station. It works by magnetically compressing plasma so that the atoms fuse. The construction costs alone of ITER are estimated at £4 billion (US$7 billion) over 10 years, and another £4 billion (US$7 billion) is expected for the 20-year operation period. However, it will be a small price to pay if nuclear fusion provides a clean, renewable energy source for the future. If nuclear fusion does become our main energy source, it is believed that greenhouse gases will almost disappear and one day it might also be used to generate vehicle fuels cleanly. Surely this is the answer to all our dreams!

According to ITER's long-term objective, the aim of this fusion research is *"to harness the nuclear energy provided by the fusion of light atoms to help meet [hu]mankind's future energy needs. This research, which is carried out by scientists from all over the word, has made tremendous progress over the last decades. The fusion community is now ready to take the next step, and have together designed the international ITER experiment. The aim of ITER is to show fusion could be used to generate electrical power, and to gain the necessary data to design and operate the first electricity-producing plant".* Source: http://www.iter.org/a/index_nav_1.htm

China's first successful test in 2006 of an experimental fusion reaction was at this facility in Anhui province.

The future of nuclear research

Just 100 years ago, scientists could never have dreamed of what atoms held in store. In another hundred years, just imagine what nuclear energy might make possible. By the middle of the next century, the world's population is likely to be double what it is now, and energy demands are predicted to triple, particularly as industry grows in economically developing countries. Supplies of fossil fuel are sure to run out, and we already know how burning such fuel damages the planet with carbon pollution.

If fossil fuels can be replaced with deuterium from the oceans, there will be enough to fuel advanced fusion reactors for millions of years. Plus, the waste product from a deuterium-tritium fusion reactor is just harmless helium.

Although solar power, wind power, and other renewable forms of energy will be important in the future, they will be unable to meet the energy demands of an industrialized world on their own. More nuclear fission power stations are likely to be built in the short term to provide energy, but there is still the problem of high-level radioactive waste.

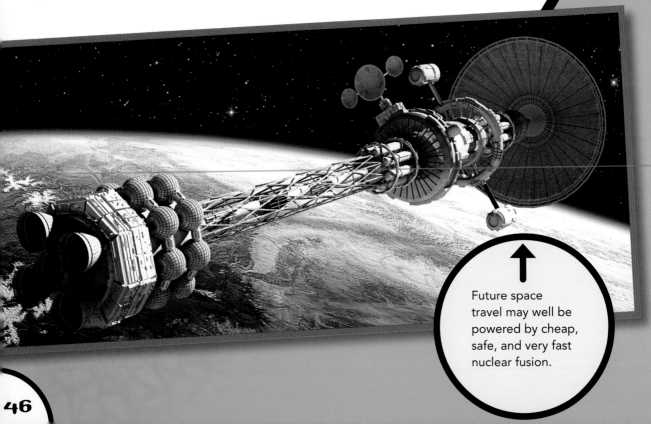

Future space travel may well be powered by cheap, safe, and very fast nuclear fusion.

Risks and hopes

The arguments about nuclear energy will doubtless continue because, as well as all the opportunities it promises, there are still serious threats. Many people are rightly concerned about its disadvantages:

- toxic radioactivity – waste for generations to come
- nuclear weapons – the fear that more countries will develop nuclear bombs
- accidents – radiation leaks from mistakes, misuse, or terrorist threats.

On the other hand, nuclear energy could help us to solve some of the big problems that face Earth in the 21st century:

- Carbon emissions and climate change – nuclear energy can make a big difference to the reduction of global warming.
- World health – nuclear energy is already being used to treat cancer and other serious diseases.
- Malaria – this disease kills over one million people each year, mainly children in the world's poorest countries. Mosquitoes with the malaria parasite bite people and infect them. Nuclear energy is being used to control the billions of mosquitoes in Africa. Scientists sterilize female mosquitoes with ionizing radiation in order to reduce the number of breeding insects.
- Drought and starvation – nuclear energy could ease drought by turning seawater into freshwater in floating power plants. Radiation is already being used as a pesticide, which could prevent crops from being devastated by pests and reduce the chance of starvation for many people.
- World poverty – millions of people in the world live in homes without electricity. If nuclear fusion can make cheap energy possible, everyone might have electricity.

Who knows what is in store for Earth in the future? A baby born today will experience a very different world from the one that we see now – and nuclear energy is likely to make up a lot of that difference. Undoubtedly, nuclear science still has many more secrets to reveal. To ensure that tomorrow's children grow up in a safe, clean, and sustainable world, nuclear science has some big challenges to solve. Our future depends on the answers, so science really will make a difference. And after all, what could possibly matter more?

Facts and figures

Nuclear timeline

1895	Wilhelm Röntgen, German physicist, discovers X-rays.
1896	Antoine Henri Becquerel, French physicist, discovers natural radiography.
1898	Marie Curie, Polish-born physicist, discovers the radioactive elements radium and polonium.
1905	German-born physicist Albert Einstein publishes his theory that matter is a form of energy and that mass and energy are related.
1911	New Zealand-born physicist Ernest Rutherford announces his discovery of the nucleus of the atom.
1932	James Chadwick, British physicist, discovers the neutron.
1938	German chemists, Otto Hahn and Fritz Strassmann, produce the elements barium and krypton by bombarding uranium with neutrons.
1939	Austrian physicists, Lise Meitner and Otto Frisch, show that Hahn and Strassmann had produced the first known artificially created reaction.
1942	A group of scientists, headed by the Italian-born physicist Enrico Fermi, produce the world's first artificially created chain reaction at the University of Chicago, USA. The Manhattan Project is formed in the USA to build the atomic bomb for use in World War II.
1945	The United States explodes the first atomic bomb on Hiroshima, Japan, and three days later drops another one on Nagasaki, Japan. World War II ends less than two weeks later when Japan surrenders.
1946	Congress establishes the atomic energy commission to control nuclear energy development in the USA.
1949	The Soviet Union detonates its first atomic device.
1952	The USA explodes its first hydrogen bomb (H-bomb) using nuclear fusion at Eniwetok, a small island in the Pacific Ocean.
1953	The first nuclear-powered submarine, *USS Nautilus*, is launched.

1956	The first full-scale nuclear power plant begins operations at Calder Hall in Cumbria, UK.
1957	The United Nations establishes the International Atomic Energy Agency to promote the peaceful use of nuclear energy. The first U.S. nuclear power plant opens in Shippingport, Pennsylvania.
1962	Canada's first full-scale nuclear power plant begins to produce electricity in Rolphton, Ontario.
1964	The U.S. Navy sends three nuclear-powered surface ships around the world to show the ability of nuclear-powered ships to operate away from shore bases.
1977	A major accident occurs at U.S. Three Mile Island nuclear plant, Pennsylvania. No one is directly injured but thousands are evacuated. It causes a public scare and concerns from the accident lead to many safety improvements for the nuclear power industry in the U.S.
1986	The world's worst nuclear power accident happens at the Chernobyl plant in the former USSR (now Ukraine).
2002	The oldest nuclear power plant in the world, Obninsk in Russia, closes down its sole reactor. Nuclear power provides about 16 percent of the world's electricity.
2004	Scotland closes the Chapelcross nuclear power station, one of the world's oldest plants. Lithuania, the world's most nuclear-dependent nation, shuts down many of its nuclear reactors of the same design as the reactors at Chernobyl. Poland begins to build the nation's first nuclear power plant.
2008	The International Thermonuclear Experimental Reactor (ITER) project, to develop nuclear fusion, signs an agreement with the European Organization for Nuclear Research (CERN). It agrees to co-operate on research and technology for developing nuclear fusion over the next 20 years.

Worldwide nuclear electricity

Nuclear power continues to increase steadily around the world. There are about 30 reactors under construction in 12 countries. Most new reactors being planned are in Asia, Europe, the USA, and Russia. Upgrading the technology and increasing the capacity is improving the performance of many existing nuclear reactors.

Nuclear-powered electricity is expected to be even more significant in the future.

Top 10 producers of nuclear electricity in 2007

Country	Amount of nuclear electricity produced (TWh*)
USA	807.0
France	420.1
Japan	267.3
Russia	148.0
South Korea	136.6
Germany	133.2
Canada	88.2
Ukraine	87.2
Sweden	64.3
China	59.3

*TWh = Terawatts per hour

Source: http://www.world-nuclear.org/info/nshare.html?terms=production+by+country

Nuclear power plants in operation or under construction, April 2008

Country	Plants in operation	Plants under construction	Country	Plants in operation	Plants under construction
Argentina	2	1	Mexico	2	0
Armenia	1	0	Netherlands	1	0
Belgium	7	0	Pakistan	2	1
Brazil	2	0	Romania	2	0
Bulgaria	2	2	Russian Federation	31	7
Canada	18	0			
China	11	6	Slovakian Republic	5	0
Czech Republic	6	0	Slovenia	1	0
Finland	4	1	South Africa	2	0
France	59	1	Spain	8	0
Germany	17	0	Sweden	10	0
Hungary	4	0	Switzerland	5	0
India	17	6	Taiwan	6	2
Iran	0	1	Ukraine	15	2
Japan	55	1	United Kingdom	19	0
Korea, Republic of	20	3			
Lithuania	1	0	USA	104	1
			Total	**439**	**35**

Source : http://www.euronuclear.org/info/encyclopedia/n/ nuclear-power-plant-world-wide.htm

Find out more

Books

Energy Debate: Nuclear Power, Ewan McLeish (Hodder Wayland, 2007)

Future Energy, Julie Richards (Macmillan World Library, 2007)

Nuclear Energy (Fuelling the Future), Chris Oxlade and Elizabeth Raum
(Heinemann Library, 2008)

Nuclear Power (Energy Sources), Neil Morris (Franklin Watts Ltd, 2006)

What Do You Think? Is Nuclear Power Safe?, John Meany
(Heinemann Library, 2008)

Why Science Matters: Predicting the Effects of Climate Change,
John Townsend (Heinemann Library, 2008)

Websites

- http://science.howstuffworks.com/nuclear.htm
  See how nuclear radiation works.

- http://www.chem4kids.com
  Learn about the science of atoms, and take a quiz on atom structure.

- http://www.physics4kids.com/files/mod_fusion.html
  Handy descriptions to help you remember the difference between
  fission and fusion.

- http://www.iter.org/index.htm
  Latest news from the International Thermonuclear Experimental
  Reactor website.

- http://www.world-nuclear.org/
  Latest information from the World Nuclear Association.

Topics for further study

- Alternative energy sources and renewable energy.

- The electromagnetic spectrum.

- Nuclear building plans in your country.

- Latest developments in nuclear medicine.

- Radon gas hot-spots around the country.

- Locate a nuclear power plant that allows public visits.

- Find out about nuclear accidents, such as Chernobyl, and how scientists disagree about the effects.

- Find out which nuclear news stories are making the headlines.

- Discuss the safety of nuclear power with a friend (try looking at the websites of Greenpeace or Friends of the Earth).

- Discuss nuclear weapons with a friend, and together decide whether they are a deterrent against war, or not.

- Discuss global warming with a friend, and decide whether or not you think nuclear energy is the best way to cut down on carbon emissions.

Glossary

antioxidant   substance such as vitamins in food, thought to protect body cells from damage

atom   smallest component of an element and a potential source of vast energy

bedrock   solid rock lying under the soil, plants, and surface materials

chain reaction   nuclear reaction producing energy causes further reactions of the same kind

cosmic rays   high energy charged particles from outer space that travel almost as fast as light, striking Earth

DNA   acids in body cell nuclei, which are the chemical basis of heredity and genetic codes

electron   particle with a negative charge of electricity that travels around the nucleus of an atom

element   substance made up of atoms of only one kind

fission   splitting of an atomic nucleus resulting in the release of large amounts of energy

fossil fuel   fuel (coal, oil, or natural gas) that is formed in the earth from plant or animal remains

hypothesis   idea based on observations without experimental evidence

immune system   body's system of antibodies that protect against disease and infection

ion   electrically charged atom as a result of having lost or gained one or more electrons

ionizing   give an atom or group of atoms a net electric charge by adding or subtracting electrons

isotope   forms of the same element that have equal numbers of protons, but different numbers of neutrons

mass   amount of matter in a body

mass spectrometer   instrument that spreads particles or radiation into an ordered sequence by mass

meltdown   accidental melting of the core of a nuclear reactor

mill tailings   rock and other materials removed when minerals are mined

molten   melted into liquid by very great heat

NASA   USA's space programme – National Aeronautics and Space Administration

neutron   atomic particle found in all known atomic nuclei except the hydrogen nucleus

Nobel Prize   annual prize for the encouragement of people who work for the interests of humanity

nuclear fusion   joining of atomic nuclei to release great quantities of energy

nuclear reaction   any reaction that involves a change in the nucleus of an atom

nucleus   (plural nuclei) central part of an atom

ore   material that contains a metal, often found in rocks

plasma   charged particles similar to gas, but good conductors of electricity and affected by magnetic field

plutonium   element produced from uranium as a result of the fission process, used as a nuclear fuel

propulsion   action or process of powering or propelling

proton   atomic particle that occurs in the nucleus of every atom and carries a positive charge

quark   particles that are believed to be part of protons or neutrons

radiation   energy that is transmitted in the form of rays, waves, or particles

radioactive   giving off rays of energy or particles by the breaking apart of atoms of elements, such as uranium

radioactivity   breakdown or decay of the nuclei of atoms by the release of particles

radiology   branch of medicine using radiation energy (as X-rays) or radioactive material and various imaging techniques to diagnose and treat disease

radium   radioactive white metallic element that occurs in very small quantities in minerals

radon   chemically inert radioactive gaseous element produced by the breaking apart of radium atoms

reactor   machine for the controlled release of heat from a nuclear reaction

spectrometry   technique used to analyze or identify substances using the wavelength spectrum either emitted or absorbed

tokamak   machine producing a magnetic field for confining a plasma. It is one of several types of magnetic confinement devices for producing fusion energy.

tsunami   giant sea wave produced by an earthquake or volcanic eruption under the sea

tumour   an abnormal mass of tissue that grows inside the body and may be caused by cancerous cells

turbine   engine with a central driving shaft that has blades spun around by the pressure of water, steam, or gases

yellowcake   fine powder milled uranium oxide (U_3O_8) which is processed into uranium hexaflouride (UF_6) in the manufacture of nuclear fuel

Index